John Ciardi

The Hopeful Trout
and
Other
Limericks

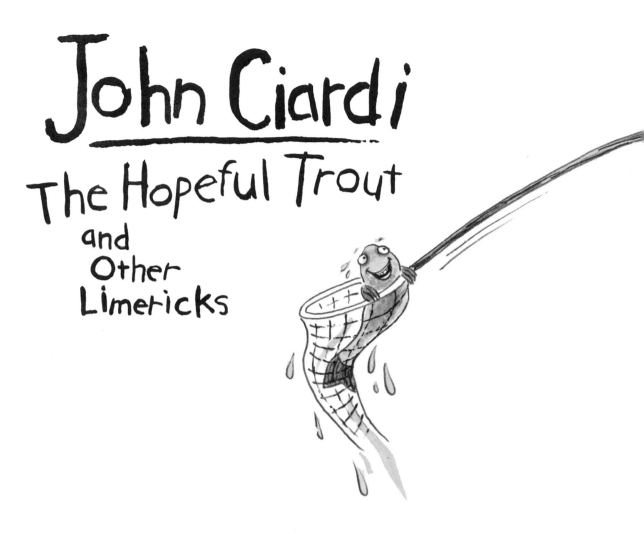

illustrated by Susan Meddaugh

Houghton Mifflin Company   Boston 1989

Also by John Ciardi:
Doodle Soup
Fast and Slow
I Met a Man

Library of Congress Cataloging-in-Publication Data

Ciardi, John
   The hopeful trout and other limericks/by John Ciardi;
illustrated by Susan Meddaugh.
         p.   cm.
   Summary: A collection of limericks about such characters as the
Elephant Boy, the fast fiddler from Middletown, and the silly old
skinflint named Quince.
   ISBN 0-395-43606-0
   1. Limericks. 2. Children's poetry, American. [1. Limericks.
2. Humorous poetry. 3. American poetry.] I. Meddaugh, Susan, ill.
II. Title.
PS3505.I27H65 1989   87-23587
811'.52—dc19   CIP
                            AC

Text © 1989 by Myra J. Ciardi
Illustrations © 1989 by Susan Meddaugh

Printed in the United States of America

P 10 9 8 7 6 5 4 3 2 1

I. Sometimes Even Parents Win

Keeping Busy Is Better Than Nothing

There was a young lady named Sue
Who had nothing whatever to do
    And who did it so badly
    I thought she would gladly
Have stopped long before she was through.

The Elephant Boy

There once was a boy with a nose
Right in front of his face. I suppose
    That's where noses belong,
    But unless I am wrong,
His really looked more like a hose.

The Thingamajig

There once was a Thingamajig —
Like a Whatsis, but three times as big.
    When it first came in view,
    It looked something like you
But it stayed and turned into a pig!

Goodbye Please

I once knew a word I forget
That means "I am sorry we met
   And I wish you the same."
   It sounds like your name
But I haven't remembered *that* yet.

When You Are There at All, That Is

There once was a Feeble so few
It took ten of him just to make two.
  Even then, what you got
  Didn't look like a lot
Though it did look a little like you.

Sometimes Even Parents Win

There was a young lady from Gloucester
Who complained that her parents both bossed her,
    So she ran off to Maine.
    Did her parents complain?
Not at all — they were glad to have lost her.

There Seems to Be a Problem

I really don't know about Jim.
When he comes to our farm for a swim,
    The fish, as a rule,
    Jump out of the pool.
Is there something the matter with him?

Be Kind to Dumb Animals

There once was an ape in a zoo
Who looked out through the bars and saw — YOU!
    Do you think it's fair
      To give poor apes a scare?
I think it's a mean thing to do!

II. It Came from Outer Space

The Hopeful Trout (Poor Fish!)

There once was a trout on a plate
Who thought, "Was it something I ate
    That brought on this dream?
    I'll be back in the stream
When it's over. Till then, I'll just wait."

It Came from Outer Space

There once was a Martian named Zed
With antennae all over his head.
     He sent out a lot
     Of di-di-dash-dot
But nobody knows what he said.

The Chow Hound

I once had a flea hound named Dizzy.
When people would ask, "What breed is he?"
    I would say, "I don't know,
      But whenever we go
To the meat market, his kind gets busy."

The Music Master

"My sons," said a Glurk slurping soup,
"We would make a fine musical group.
    Put your spoon to your lip
    And slurp when you sip,
But don't spill. Like this, children — Oop!"

Home Sweet Home

A flea on a pooch doesn't care
Which part it is crossing to where.
    Like mud to a frog,
    Any part of a dog
Suits a flea, and it's glad to be there.

Paying through the Nose

There once was a bear in a tree
Eating honey. But honey's not free.
      Bees don't give it away.
      You may have to pay
Through the nose. Ask the next bear you see.

The Dinner

The Price

That Fish Was Just Too Fussy

I said to a fish in the lake,
"I have worms, peas, and chocolate cake.
    Would you care for a bite?"
    Said the fish, "I just might,
But I think it would be a mistake."

Stop Squirming!

A nervous young worm once got twisted
In a knot that completely resisted
    All attempts to untie it.
    I hope you don't try it
Or you may end up ceased and desisted!

The Halloween House

I'm told there's a Green Thing in there.
And the sign on the gate says BEWARE!
    But of course it's not true.
    That's why I'm sending you
To sneak in and find out — *but take care!*

III. He Was Brave, But Not for Long

Win Some, Lose Some

There was a brave hunter named Paul
Who strangled nine grizzlies one fall.
    Nine is such a good score,
    He tried for one more.
But he lost. Well, you can't win them all!

Speedy Sam

Speedy Sam, while exploring a cave,
Had what I call a very close shave.
  He stepped on a bear
   That had dozed off in there.
I am glad he was faster than brave!

Friendship

There once were two back-country geezers
Who got porcupine quills in their sneezers.
    They sat beak to beak
    For more than a week
Working over each other with tweezers.

They Had a Point to Make

Some hornets one day in a nest
Saw a boy who was doing his best
    To play them a trick
    With a rather short stick
And came out to . . . well, you know the rest!

April Fool

At show-and-tell time yesterday
I brought my pet skunk. Sad to say,
    Though it had been well taught
    Not to spray, it forgot.
Now we can't use the schoolhouse till May.

He Was Brave, but Not for Long

There was a brave hunter named Fred
Who used to kick moose in the head.
    He used to chase bears
    Right into their lairs.
When I last heard, he used to be dead.

About Learning Things the Hard Way

There was a young fellow named Clive
Who tried to peek into a hive.
    What he wanted to see is
    How busy a bee is.
Now he knows, but he's barely alive.

HIVE   CLIVE

IV. Iron Men and Wooden Ships

Iron Men and Wooden Ships

Said a salty old skipper from Wales,
"Number one, it's all right to chew nails.
    It impresses the crew,
    It impresses me, too.
But stop spitting holes in the sails!"

The Poor Boy Was Wrong

There was a young fellow named Sid
Who thought he knew more than he did.
    He thought that a shark
    Would turn tail if you bark.
So he swam out to try it — poor kid!

The Mystery

There was a young fellow named Chet
Who swam out to sea on a bet.
    Did he win? I don't know:
    That was two months ago
And we haven't caught sight of him yet.

Ho-Hum

There once was an oyster whose head
Was never once raised from his bed.
    "What a very dull life
    We live!" said his wife.
"Perhaps. But I like it," he said.

Willis C. Sick

There was a young man on a ship
Who counted each pitch and each dip,
    Each roll and each yaw,
    Each sea and each saw
On a twenty-six-thousand-mile trip.

V. Heights Made Him Dizzy

Rest in Peace

A silly old skinflint named Quince
Used up all his life skinning flints.
    When the last flint was skun
    He said, "Well, that's done!"
And dropped dead — which he's been ever since.

Like a Fire-Eating Dragon

There was a young chow hound named Billy
Who ate six whole bowls of hot chili.
    As his temperature rose,
    Steam shot from his nose,
Which I think made him look rather silly!

Heights Made Him Dizzy

There was a young fellow so frail
He could fly on a kite — as the tail.
    That gave him a view
    From Maine to Peru.
But when he looked down he turned pale!

He Saved a Lot of Time by Not Working

South of Nome there's a farmer I know
Whose fields are all covered with snow
    From October to May
    When the stuff melts away
Leaving just time for nothing to grow.

OINK

Serves Him Right

There was an old man on a hill
Who said to the birds, "Oh, be still!"
    One bird, just for that,
    Built a nest in his hat
And pecked both his ears with its bill.

All Right, Do It Your Way!

Sam the soup maker tried to fry ice
In a colander. When once or twice
    I stopped by to say,
     "You'll get no soup that way,"
He snarled, "I don't need your advice!"

The Fast Fiddler

There was a fast fiddler from Middletown
Who fiddled hi-diddle-dee-diddle-down.
    As his foot kept on tapping
    His strings kept on snapping
Ping-ping-ping, till he put his old fiddle down.

And They Met in the Middle

There was a young fellow named Pete
Who wasn't what I would call neat.
      One rumple worked down
      From the top of his crown,
And another worked up from his feet.

Do You Know Anyone Like Him?

There was a young fellow named Paul
Who didn't like most things at all.
    What he liked was to take
    Whatever would break
And break it — and then sit and bawl!

The Thinker

There was a young fellow who thought
Very little, but thought it a lot.
    Then at long last he knew
    What he wanted to do,
But before he could start, he forgot.